Three Little Plays

Other Starfall Books
by Margaret Hillert

Happy Mother's Day, Dear Dragon
Not Too Little to Help
Penguin, Penguin
The No-Tail Cat

This book is part of the
"I'm Reading!" fluent reading sequence
featured on

www.**starfall**.com

This series is designed to encourage reading
fluency. It allows children to achieve mastery
and confidence by reading substantial books
(both fiction and non-fiction) that use a
limited vocabulary of sight words. "Step 1"
refers to the easiest group of books in this series.
It can be read after, or at the same time as,
Starfall's well-known Learn-to-Read phonics
series featuring Zac the Rat™ and other tales.

Three Little Plays

by Margaret Hillert

For the earliest reader

Illustrated by Craig Deeley and Dale Beisel

Starfall™
www.starfall.com

ISBN: 1-59577-018-6

Starfall Publications
P.O. Box 359, Boulder, Colorado 80306

Contents

Dog and Cat

A Play

Players:

DOG

CAT

DOG: Go away, Cat.

Go away.

I do not want you here.

CAT: Why not?

DOG: You do not look like me.

You look funny.

I do not like you.

CAT: You look funny, too.

I will go away.

I do not want to play

with you.

DOG: Cat went away.

That is good.

Now I can have fun.

I can run and play.

I can do what I want.

DOG: This is funny.

I can do what I want,

but I am not happy.

DOG: Where are you, Little Cat?
I want you.
Come here. Come here.

CAT: Why, Dog?
Why do you want me?

DOG: I want to play with you.
      You do not look funny.
      You look like you, and
      I like you that way.

CAT: That is good, Dog.
      I like you, too.
      I like to play with you.

Guess, ? Guess

A Play

Players:

BOY

GIRL

BOY: What do you have?

I want to look at it.

GIRL: No, no.

You can not look.

Guess, guess.

BOY: Is it something little?

Is it something big?

GIRL: It is little.

Oh, yes. It is little.

Guess, guess.

BOY: Is it something red?
       Is it something yellow?

GIRL: Yes, yes.
       It is red AND yellow.
       Go on. Go on.

BOY: Can you eat it?

Is it good to eat?

GIRL: No, no.

You can not eat it.

BOY: Can you play with it?

Is it something to play with?

GIRL: Yes, you can play with it,

but what is it?

You have to guess.

BOY: Is it a car?

A little car to play with?

GIRL: No, it is not a car.

That is not it.

BOY: What is it?

              What is it?

              I can not guess.

GIRL: It is TWO cars.

Two little cars.

One for you and one for me.

Now we can play and have

fun.

Cookies

A Play

Players:

MOTHER: Come here.
            Come here.
            Run, run, run.
            I want you.

BOY and GIRL: What for, Mother?

Why do you want us?

MOTHER: I want you to help me.
I will make cookies,
and you can help me.

BOY and GIRL: Oh, boy!

What fun!

We like to do this.

GIRL: I will make one look
like a cat.

BOY: I can make one look
like a dog.

MOTHER: Now – here they go.

In here.

In here.

BOY: And now – into us!
        One in me.
        And one in you.

GIRL: We like to help you, Mother.
        And we like to eat cookies.

About the Author

Margaret Hillert wrote her first poem when she was eight years old. At eighty-five she's still writing books and poems for children and adults all around the world.

Margaret knows what children like to read because she was a first-grade teacher for 34 years. She loves to visit her local library and read to children.

The Women's National Book Association honored Margaret in 1993 for writing wonderful children's books. But she says her BIGGEST reward has been teaching so many children how to read!

Vocabulary - 69 Words

a	fun	make	too
am	funny	me	two
and	girl	mother	us
are	go	no	want
at	good	not	way
away	guess	now	we
big	happy	oh	went
boy	have	on	what
but	help	one	where
can	here	play	why
car(s)	I	players	will
cat	in	red	with
come	into	run	yellow
cookies	is	something	yes
do	it	that	you
dog	like	they	
eat	little	this	
for	look	to	